Italian Air / Radiant Days

Neil Leadbeater

Copyright© 2024 Neil Leadbeater
ISBN: 978-81-19654-50-5

First Edition: 2024
Rs. 200/-

Cyberwit.net
HIG 45 Kaushambi Kunj, Kalindipuram
Allahabad - 211011 (U.P.) India
http://www.cyberwit.net
Tel: +(91) 9415091004
E-mail: info@cyberwit.net

No part of this book may be reproduced or transmitted in any form or by any means, electronic, mechanical, photocopying, or otherwise, without the express written consent of Neil Leadbeater.

Printed at Repro India Limited.

For Jane

Acknowledgements

I am grateful to the editors of the following publications in which some of these poems, a few in earlier versions, first appeared or are forthcoming: *Dreich* (UK), *Fire* (UK), *ibid* (UK), *Ink Pantry* (UK), *Littoral Magazine* (UK), *North of Oxford* (USA), *Orizont Literar Contemporan* (Romania) and *Poetry Atlas* (USA).

I am also indebted to Shutta Crum and Caroline Gill for their careful reading of my original manuscript and supporting commentary and to members of The Burgh Poets, Stirling, for comments on earlier drafts of specific poems. It has been a pleasure to share poetry with you all.

Contents

I: The Slipping Forecast

The Slipping Forecast

This poem was issued at 0500 hrs, GMT.
on Friday 19th January 2024

There are warnings of fractures
in North Utsire and South Utsire
winds southeasterly
becoming cyclonic
veering northerly later.
Severe gale 9 to storm force 10.
Enough to reel you off your feet
for a hard landing on deck.
Rain intermittent.
Moderate to poor.
Pain expected later.

Fracture

A poem that is

out of alignment

is one that does not sing.

II: Italian Air / Radiant Days

A Leading Question

Was the Leaning Tower of Pisa built to lean on purpose
or was it a mistake?

Soft ground was the determining factor.
Unable to hold its structured weight
unstable soil set its destiny on a southern tilt
sloping over time.
Bonanno Pisano was not acquainted with ground engineering
his head was too much taken up with classical capitals
and blind arches
to notice any difference.

Facts I Did Not Know about The Leaning Tower of Pisa

1. That it leant north before leaning south
(the building changed its mind)
2. That it never used to lean at all
3. That it only leant when it put on weight
4. That its feet found fault with the ground
5. That Galileo Galilei used it for experiments
6. That Benito Mussolini ruined it
7. That 'Pisa' means 'marshy land'
8. That it is not the only leaning tower in Pisa

According to Computers, the Tower should have Toppled

Let's just say that by 1990
the tower was leaning a whole 5.5 degrees,
but computer models show
that it should have fallen at 5.44 degrees,
so we are now 0.06 degrees
over the limit
and still standing.
Each day it is learning to defy the laws of gravity
a bell tower in the Field of Miracles
16 feet off perpendicular.

Who Put the Lean in the Tower of Pisa?

Maybe it was the tower itself.
At first it was almost imperceptible:
about three-fourths of an inch per year.
Nothing you could see with the naked eye.

Its limbs longed to sink
into a cushion of repose.

It just wanted
to slip off its shoes
in order to rest its feet.

Surface Tension

VeNeZiA RiDiNg ThE WaVeS

Recent studies suggest that Venice is sinking at a rate of about 1 to 2 mm a year, and if it keeps this up over the next 20 years, it will sink by around 80 mm relative to sea level. Many climate experts suggest that Venice could sink by 2100.

Il Prete Rosso Running

It seems unseemly for a priest to run. Surely he is better seen
making his way with dignified steps from one station to another
but Nike and running shorts have the upper hand
mornings at ten
as he pounds the pavement shopfronts
shunning tramezzino sandwiches
and Alperol low-proof liquor,
shelves of Illy's red-striped tins,
tailor dummies rooted to the spot
in chambray shirting and quilted jackets,
tweed accessories and Merola gloves,
wine merchants stocking up on Sicily's indigenous varietals…
none of which he sees
having his mind on the great race which is set before him
with saints in stadiums cheering him on
no time to lose from the day.

Mattioli's *Syringa vulgaris*

Brought by Busbecq from Istanbul,
we used to lie in its bushy thicket
inhaling the scent of early summers
beneath its heart-shaped leaves.
Each colour carried its own specifics:
white for purity and innocence,
purple for matters religious
blue for peace and contentment.

Nothing compares
with the springtime awakening
of a syringarium in bloom.

'Harper's Bazaar named it the colour of 2018'

Its pastel tones are white whorls
of shaving cream.

Its purple the shade of Byzantine Emperors
Roman togas
royalty.

Its pink tint
points to a warmer clime.

It pairs well with royal weddings.
historic mid-term elections
and a very American addition
to the British royal family.

All this in a year
when all the talk in the world of fashion
is of boots with suits,
modern workwear, faux fur,
dark denim, leopard print:
mauve | lavender | lilac.

Lilacs by Other Names

Angel White

packs a powerful scent.
Its pure white clusters
that frothy look you sometimes get
on the top of a café latte.

Beauty of Moscow

pink pearl-like buds opening into
gorgeous double-whites.
Bees welcome.

Congo

Wine-red flowers
enough to pull the butterflies
into its glassy depths.

Lavender Lady

Strolling through the morning air
Dressed in purple
a world leader in beauty.

Paolo Boccone's *Campanula saxatilis*

In the shadow of St. Antony
patron saint of priests and travellers
Brother Silvio, much travelled,
walks through one of the oldest gardens
in the whole wide world.
In the city of Padua he lacks nothing
even though guidebooks remind us
it is 'the city of the three withouts,'
home to the café without doors
being the *Pedrocchi*
which traditionally never closed;
the meadow without grass
(the *Prato della Valle*, now a town square)
and the saint without a name
because his name goes without saying:
a 'given' that lives forever.

In the University gardens,
he'll not forget the day he found
the *trachelium*. It was almost as if
the plant had been waiting for him
to really see it for what it was,
ringing its bell-like colours
in all the rocky places –
an obligate chasmophyte
lifting its colour into a quiet clamour
head above the ground.

Michelangelo Tilli Contemplating an Orange

Whole, it is truly globular,
its lush body
a dotted surface
ready to roll
into the palm of his hand.

Sectioned into halves,
he can almost slice with precision
its succulent
marmalade segments -
scoop them into his mouth.

Barberini's Gardens on the Quirinale

In the Esquilino neighbourhood -
a multi-cultural mélange
of Asian and African stalls,
budget hotels and traditional *trattorias*
where secret alleys and archaic arches
vie with liberty buildings –
his *Giardino* of arborescent plants:
mastic, myrtle and laurel,
a *hortus conclusus*, if ever there was one,
of stone pines, fountains and statuary,
elliptical espaliers of laurel and box,
old Bourbon roses, a *Sophora japonica*
and an avenue of citrus groves –
a good place in which to meet
the Queen of the Night
whose large flowers, being shy,
only bloom after dark.

Green Spaces

In his leading landscapes, Pietro Porcinai
let nature breathe through the lungs of architecture,
glimpsed fields fully cropped
through arched colonnades,
made sure sunlight
found its way into buildings
to warm in ample measure
mosaic marble tiles.

His personal studios were glass-walled
greenhouses for the winter storage
of lemons, his green-fingered designs
for parks and gardens
numbered almost a thousand,
many for Florence alone.
Each one was an earthly paradise,
his idea of the Garden of Eden:
lawns with wild mint,
rounded river pebbles,
labyrinthine hedging, swimming pools
bordered by round slabs
of Red Verona marble,
elaborate water cisterns with trailing ivy,
Pinnochio park stones...
his cultural vision global.

Petrarch's Feet

Students of podiatry learn human anatomy and physiology,
conditions musculoskeletal,
gait, footwear and more
but Petrarch repeatedly applied himself
to the challenge of exploring fourteen lines
written in iambic pentameters -
so walk me through Rima 190
the one about the white doe
glimpsed between two rivers
in the shade of a laurel at sunrise
and let me gloss over a line of verse
with five metrical feet
before I topple into the b(r)ook
and the doe disappears from sight.

Monteverdi's Gestures

Gesture. *n.*

-a movement of the body, especially a hand or the head
to express an idea or a meaning.
-an action performed to convey a feeling or intention.

A player of viols, his fingers would have fled
through five to seven strings,
positioned upright
like the modern cello
he'd exult in its soft sonority.

In *Combattimento di Tancredi e Clorinda*
his plucked notes made a satisfying
percussive sound
that had not been heard before.

The new genre surprised us all.

His styles of composition –
the heritage of Renaissance polyphony
and the new basso continuo
belonging to the Baroque –
were gestures that unfolded
to those in the know.

His secular madrigals
redefined the mould,

pushing the boundaries
into new territory.

Everything he did
pointed in a new direction.

Trieste I

In the crook of Italy,
the coffee capital of Illy and Hausbrandt,
that dark rich brew of a city
huddled in a demitasse cup -
home of Italian ceramics,
Istrian truffles and old world grandeur,
architecture comes with a mixed message:
Mitteleuropa with mansard windows
meets full-on Italian Liberty style
where a gale force katabatic wind
cups its resonance round open squares
fresh off the ridge of Europe.

Trieste II

Those glory days of Belle Époch posters, tariff lists and liners
reminders of an eclectic era from the shipyards of old
is where East meets West and everyone shouts
'Trieste is ours': a landscape in limbo –
the last ring on the rail
that held up the Iron Curtain –
a deep-water port of Latin, Slavic and German cultures
and everywhere the sea, the blue-dazed beauty of it,
dazzling stars.

Swing by for a week
and you might just stay forever.

Italian Brands

Ferrari

This horse is more than prancing.
Bristling with energy
every fibre in its sleek body
dreams of leaving that yellow rectangle,
to race with the traffic
out of Modena
when the green light comes.

Olivetti

Choosing the right signage
they gave it that initial 'O' of surprise
and then let all the other letters
revert to type.

Italia '90

'Ciao', fully flagged and patriotic
heads the ball to the winning goal:

a victory for postmodern Italy.

Lamborghini

Golden bull on a black shield
symbol of power and strength:
all muscle, head lowered,
ready for action NOW.

Renzo Piano's Iconic Designs

Even the word 'rubble' earned his respect.
To him it was simply 'masonry not yet fully dressed'.
It held possibilities, the natural shape of it,
squared, coursed or snecked,
could be re-fashioned into something chic
attracting the eyes of photographers
all over the globe.
The buildings he created were statements
in their own right: iconic structures
of glass and steel. He strove to push the boundaries
of what was possible into a new reality.
They had a lightness of touch, a simplicity
and a transparency about them
that belied their architectural complexity.
His green roofs and energy-efficient systems
are very much of our time.
In him, modern aesthetic shakes hands
with historic backdrop:
the next generation is born.

Running Late

The girls at the *Ospidale* are used to it by now
and wait obediently for the maestro.
They know that he who insists on perfect timing
when it comes to making music
is sometimes wide of the metronome.
Composing a work like *La Stravaganza*
stops all the clocks inside him.
Working with so many time signatures
they will forgive him for his lateness.

You have to make room for inspiration
and take it when it comes.

L'estro armonico

In Naples, strolling down a side-street
he sees the master craftsmen
labouring at their work,
observes how their fingers are already perfecting
soundboards for their art,
moving from one instrument
to the next,
a harmonious inspiration filled with possibility.
No time to lose, he sets his staves
with dots, minims and quavers,
remembers to tell his girls that All Cows Eat Grass
and adds the mandolin with its dulcet tones
to his repertoire of concertos
for two, three and four violins,
viola d'amore, 'cello,
longitudinal and transverse flutes,
oboe and bassoon.
Soon the whole neighbourhood is talking,
word is getting around:
Viva, Viva Vivaldi!

Vivaldi in Four Seasons

Spring

Expect rain in most places, snow
in the mountains but the temperature
will be comfortable enough.
May is the prettiest month
before the summer explodes with tourists.
Outdoor concerts will be starting soon.
Time to exult in eggshells
to break open an octave of joy.
On the *Festa della Donna*
he brings yellow mimosas
to the mistress in his life,
composes his sonatas for violin
and basso continuo, his Contest
between Harmony and Invention.

Summer

June to August is hot and humid
with lean patches of rain. Time
to work on *Orlando Furioso*
or *La Cetra*
to savour the spectacle
of chivalry,
to observe the days
of patron saints.

Autumn

November is the rainiest month.
Days are short and the weather variable
but the autumn colours –
a palette of orange, yellow and gold –
more than make up
as he breathes in woodland scents
composing *Aristide*
immersed in a sea of leaves.

Winter

The Italians have flocked to the Alps.
Left to its own devices, the country
takes on a distinctive charm
with quieter cities and sights.
He looks forward, in his old age,
to the Christmas markets
in Trento and Trieste,
masked balls in February,
opera in the spring.

Italian Inventions

See how that Cristofori piano, newly-delivered,
redefines the room: its sleek presence,
lid half raised, in welcome.

You walk towards it with reverence. All your movements
are choreographed like ballet round the room.

On the side-table there is a radio. Antonio Meucci's
wireless telegraphy.

A barometer registers 29.80 inches of mercury.
Thank you Torricelli. Expect warm air and rain.

Yesterday's *La Republica* lies on the chair –
circulation, when I last looked, 116,752, established 1976 –
it's come a long way since the *Gazette of Venice* in 1566.

On the tray, one of Alfonso Bialetti's octagonal Moka Pots
ideal for stove-top brewing.

Ravizzi's typewriter sits on the desk. A sheet of paper
with this poem in it awaits the last three lines.

You put on your glasses, pick up the phone
speak to the oldest bank in the world –
pay for that piano.

Stopping for Lunch in Vipiteno

Twinned with Kitzbühel, the city boasts two names:
Sterzing / Vipiteno –
a place more Austrian than Italian,
snuggled by mountains
in the province of Bolzano,
South Tyrol.

Coming out of Café Mondschein
where the menu is still in German,
we walk beneath the Tower of Twelve
known for its midday chimes.

A firebreak between two worlds
with views into the hills.

III: From *A Medieval Bestiary*

The Glow Worm

An emanation of sparks lights up the night -
Marvell's 'country comets'
that 'presage the grass's fall'.

Back then, we didn't know the meaning
of bioluminescence
or how, when we did, it would take
the romance of lanterns
right out of our lives.

Antelopes

Their long serrated horns can bring down trees,
scissor shrubs and timber
or become entangled in a bush or thicket
like Absalom whose hair got caught
in the broad branches of a giant oak
when riding his mule below.

Now in the sands of Africa
they answer to different names:
oryx, gemsbok, gnu,
impala, klipsinger, sassaby -
some 'as fierce and fell as a wolf'
adapted for survival.

The Cuckoo

It's that two-note call again
striking on the hour.
Part of me wants to know
if you are pendulum-driven:
a Midwich cuckoo
of moral ambiguity.

The Salamander

Sometimes we see you escape from a log
thrown across a fire.

We marvel at your lizard limbs,
that moist aquatic skin
with its stripes, bars, spots and blotches,
exchanging smuts of ember light
for the pitter-patter of rain.

Mayflies

Above the river

a dense cloud

of full stops

close clusters
of the order
Ephemeroptera,

shadflies,
fishflies,
aquatic naiads,

movers of nutrients,

living long enough

into the night
just to feed on air.

Centaurs

A poem in two halves

Joined at the hip, they are liminal beings
caught between two natures –
the wild offspring
of Magnesian mares
whose battles were dubbed
as struggles
between civilisation and barbarism:

gentility and savagery
jockeying for position.

The Roe Deer

Capreolus capreolus

Smaller than a stag and larger than a goat –
a billy with a diminutive suffix
that eases out arrows and seeks out herbs,
defends itself from hunters,
runs rings round trees.

The Cormorant

According to Aristotle, the cormorant is a diver that stays underwater for as long as it takes a man to walk a mile.

Think of the lungs working to order
at the slowest possible pace-

of Budimir Šobat's world record
of staying underwater -

George Orwell coming up for air.

Horseflies

Any movement in grass
will bring them out *en masse*:
March flies, dun-flies, stouts –
buzzing like chainsaws
close to the ear -
a dense skein clouding the air:
swarms that bite without warning
thirsty at all times for blood.

Behemoth

He makes his presence felt on the page

In Times New Roman 72.

No font is big enough to baptize him whole -

who drank all the water out of the Jordan
just to quench his thirst.

IV: Diversions

An exercise in skiing off-piste

Middle of the Road

Experts say that cymophane yields a pleasing opalescence.

Eye-shine from the eyes of a cat.

A single ray of white light
across a lemon disc.

Aquamarine

Everyone was head over heels

as she walked down Somersault Row

sweater by Aquascutum

love-it lipstick by Lancôme

eyewear by Carrera

1960s miniskirt

stiletto sling-back shoes

Emerald

Once she caught sight of the luna moths
alighting in handfuls from heaths and moors
she soon forgot about the emerald pendant
and thought instead
about their frail interiors –
that brief hold on life.

Ruby

Look into its brilliance
and you will see how it brims
with the red intensity of lip gloss,
its signature rouge fluorescence
a gem that really glows.

Rubies command the highest per carat price of any coloured stone.

Citrine

Greta Garbo's jewels. Tawny amber –
the thick, yellow rind of a huge, rough lemon,
Sulawesi canary flycatchers,
citrine wagtails, Bolivian warblers -
tones that range from lemon yellow
to a gorgeous shade of gold.

Obsidian

Bottle glass, coarse green, used in the making of
narrow-necked, hollow vessels
lodged in the dictionary between
obsessive-compulsive and obsolescent.

Continually counting bottles
then losing one's nerve
renders the exercise useless.

Caught in Amber

Tumble polished,
everything stalls
between RED
and GREEN:
spiders, termites,
pollen, leaves,
unable to
cross the road.

Jet

Not so much the setting that sparkles in a gem
but more a way of living
where poems travel the world over
because they're worth it.

V: London Days

In Oakwood Park

Here in the woodland of Enfield Chase
Samuel Sugden's igloo ice-well
everything falls to this:

picnics under scarlet oaks

children launching model yachts

the thud of a tennis ball over the net

a startle of finches in a line of poplars

old men on memorial benches

knuckles of gnarled bark.

Arnos Grove

In Arnos Park
it's the viaduct that catches our attention -
a brick colossus of 34 arches
strides at a diagonal
across the new-mown lawn.
where trains break out
of the Underworld
to travel like Persephone
above the Pymmes Brook.

South Acton

Here at Acton
proliferating weeds
litter the nettle bed.
Seeds of burdock
line the sun-spilt stone,
chipped brick and rank grass -
places of no name
or home.

We wait for the bell
to release the brake.

Nobody changes here.

Foxgloves fill
the pitted holes
and bits of broken
chipped off poles
lie strewn about the track.

The train shunts down
the distant line
and later

will be back.

Zoo Story

(i)

It was late August
when we took the sunlit double-decker
and asked for two returns:
one adult and one child
twelve stops to the Zoo.

Those days I had no feel for distance.
I thought the animals who had come by sea
had merely moved house as we had done
from Palmers Green to Winchmore Hill
one stop up the line.
I did not know they had to front
a whole new *terra firma*
or keep their learnt behaviours
secret in the gene pool.

(ii)

In the library there is a portrait of
    Abraham D Bartlett
First Great Superintendent of London Zoo,
    1859-1985.
You can see him in his stovepipe hat
in the imitation mountain landscape
housing the Hanuman langurs.

(iii)

In my dreams, the red livery of the
London Fire Brigade roars past sleek as
a running cheetah. And I hear the shriek
of cockatoos, wildfowl in the woodpen,
chattering monkeys aping the keepers
and the long-haul growl of a tiger

(iv)

Paradise is a return ticket to the
rainforests of Surinam, high
Arctic Tundra, South African Veldt,
a place where the climate suits all year,
somewhere they can all call home:
anywhere but here.

Early Summer in the Roding Valley

Please close the gates behind you and keep all dogs under control.

In the Roding Valley Meadows grazing cows remind us
that these were drovers' roads.
Now they are awash with flowers:
yellow loosestrife and water plantain,
stiff-growing knapweed with reddish purple heads
that push their way through a knot of bracts
into the light of day.

Beyond the near horizon
London is a heat haze
shimmering in suburbia:
Cowper's 'tight boxes, neatly sash'd'
somewhere on the edge of Essex
where 'bottled wasps' and businessmen
give way to country air.

Hainault

At first it was *Henehout* and then it was *Hyneholt.*
The name elements *higna* and *holt*
corresponding in Modern English to 'community woodland'
hints at forests on the edge of Epping:
Hatfield and Writtle, Wintry and Hainault
which I take to be the hunting grounds
of royalty enjoyed by Kings of old:
wild boar, antlered deer,
Pitter's 'bovine blare'
all the clamour of Fairlop Fair
when citizens in their thousands
would mingle in July
just to be near a well-loved oak
whose girth stretched some seventy feet
and held the weather of Hainault
deep within its rings.

www.ingramcontent.com/pod-product-compliance
Lightning Source LLC
LaVergne TN
LVHW040955150826
845672LV00002B/711

* 9 7 8 8 1 1 9 6 5 4 5 0 5 *